HEROES OF 9/11

Written by Carrie Pike

Illustrated by Annie Mears

THE BROTHERS LAST RIDE....

APPROXIMATELY 5 YEARS AFTER 9-11, I HAD THE HOUSE WATCH AND EARLY IN AFTERNOON SOMEONE KNOCKED AT THE DOOR. THE YOUNG MAN STOOD THERE HOLDING A PAPER BAG . HE HANDED IT TO ME AND SAID HE TOOK THE PICTURE AND HELD ONTO IT ALL THIS TIME, HE DID NOT SELL IT TO THE NEWS OUTLETS . HE CHERISHED IT. HE SAID IT WAS TIME, AND HE WALKED AWAY.

~LIEUTENANT FIREFIGHTER DAVID TURNER - ENGINE 54 LADDER 4 BATTALION 9

9781948804240

carriebears.com - carriebears99@gmail.com

THE MORNING WAS A NORMAL ONE
PEOPLE BUSTLING IN THE STREETS
GOING TO WORK OR DAYCARE
NOT KNOWING WHAT THEY'D SOON GREET

THE MEN THAT HIJACKED THE PLANES
INTENDED TO MAKE THEIR MARK
ATTACKING OUR COUNTRY WITH SUCH FORCE
THE SKY NOW BECOMING DARK

THE PLANES THAT FLEW TOO LOW
DESTRUCTION STRAIGHT AHEAD
COLLIDING WITH THEIR TARGETS
PEOPLE TRAPPED INSIDE WITH DREAD

SOME CLIMBED FLIGHTS AND FLIGHTS OF STAIRS
WITH HEAVY GEAR ON THEIR BACKS
TELLING PEOPLE TO RUSH ON DOWN
TO SAFETY BEFORE THE TOWER CRACKS

THESE MEN SAVE LIVES, TOO MANY TO COUNT
BUT ON THIS DREADED DAY
THOUSANDS OF PEOPLE MADE IT OUT
BECAUSE THE FDNY DIDN'T BACK AWAY
THEY WERE ON DUTY TO PROTECT AND SAVE
WITH COURAGE THEY FOUGHT STRONG
BUT TUMBLING DOWN THE DEBRIS CAME FAST
SOMETHING JUST SO WRONG

FIREFIGHTERS WHO WERE OFF DUTY
MADE THEIR WAY TO THE CITY AS FAST AS THEY COULD
PANIC AND WORRY IN THEIR SOULS
FOR THEIR BROTHERS WHO NO LONGER STOOD

DAYS AND WEEKS WOULD SOON FOLLOW

SO MANY PILES TO GO THROUGH

FAMILIES HOPEFUL THEIR DADS WOULD BE FOUND

BUT AS TIME PASSED THEY KNEW

THEY WOULDN'T HAVE THEIR DAD TO HOLD
TO SWING THEM UP IN THE SKY
HE WOULDN'T BE THERE FOR THE BIG THINGS TOO
LIKE WALKING THEM DOWN THE AISLE

ALL GAVE SOME

ENGINE 54 ✠ LADDER 4
9TH BATTALION

SOME GAVE ALL

THE COUNTRY WAS WOUNDED BY ALL THE DEATH

FAMILIES ACHING SO MUCH INSIDE

COULD WE HELP FILL IN THE HURT

PARTICULARLY FOR THESE DADS WHO TOOK THE RIDE

FIRE DEPART
CITY OF
NEW YORK

In Loving Memory of
Joseph Angelini Jr.
Ladder 4
September 11, 2001

INTO THE DANGER TO SAVE THE REST
INTO THE FIGHT AND FIRE
THEY ARE THE HEROES ABOVE ALL THE REST
WHO'S FATE WAS SO DIRE
ACROSS THE STATES SOME LADIES MET
TO PUT A PLAN IN PLACE
MAKING TEDDY BEARS TO HELP THE HURT
SOMETHING FOR FAMILIES TO EMBRACE

IN A FEW SHORT MONTHS OVER 400 BEARS
WERE MADE TO SEND FAR AWAY
SOME WERE DELIVERED IN BOXES BY MAIL
SOME HANDED IN PERSON IN ARMS TO STAY

HUGS AND TEARS AT A CHRISTMAS PARTY
AT ENGINE 54
MOMENTS OF NEW FRIENDSHIP
FOR THOSE NOT FORGOTTEN ANYMORE

FALL OF 2001, CARRIE BEARS JOINED WITH CARING CONNECTIONS (A HOPE AND COMFORT IN GRIEF PROGRAM BASED IN THE UNIVERSITY OF UTAH COLLEGE OF NURSING) TO MAKE A CARRIE BEAR FOR EACH OF THE FALLEN FDNY, NYPD AND PORT AUTHORITY OFFICERS' FAMILIES (TOTALING 412 BEARS). IT TOOK MANY VOLUNTEERS AND HELPING HANDS TO PROVIDE "SOMETHING TO HOLD ONTO" TO MEMORIALIZE THESE HEROES. WHILE BOXES AND BOXES OF CARRIE BEARS WERE SHIPPED TO RESPECTIVE FIRE HOUSES, IT WAS A PRIVILEGE TO PERSONALLY HAND DELIVER THEM TO FAMILIES OF ENGINE 54 LADDER 4 BATTALION 9 ON DECEMBER 15, 2001 – JUST IN TIME FOR THE HOLIDAYS. DAVE TURNER MADE THIS ALL POSSIBLE. HE WAS OUR POINT PERSON IN GETTING PATCHES AND ALL OF THE NAMES AND INFORMATION. I HAVE CORRESPONDED WITH DAVE OVER THE PAST 20 YEARS. EVERY 9/11 WE EXCHANGE EMAILS AND I LET HIM KNOW I HAVE NOT FORGOTTEN HIS FDNY BROTHERS. HE IS AN AMAZING PERSON AND A GOOD FRIEND. BECAUSE OF DAVE I HAVE BEEN ABLE TO GET TO KNOW THE INCREDIBLE FDNY FAMILIES.

I AM SO BLESSED TO KNOW AND LOVE THEM ALL! ~ CARRIE PIKE

DAVID TURNER (FIREFIGHTER AT ENGINE 54 LADDER 4 BATTALION 9 – MIDTOWN MANHATTAN) AND CARRIE PIKE (OWNER AND CREATOR OF CARRIE BEARS) AT THE CHRISTMAS PARTY
DECEMBER 15, 2001
DELIVERING CARRIE BEARS
TO THE FDNY FAMILIES.

DAVE TURNER & CARRIE PIKE
SEPTEMBER 11, 2021 – TWENTY YEARS LATER

ABOUT THE AUTHOR

CARRIE PIKE RESIDES IN SALT LAKE CITY WITH HER HUSBAND AND FIVE SONS. IN ADDITION TO HER WORK IN CREATING CARRIE BEARS IN 1999, CARRIE HAS ALSO SPENT THE PAST 30 YEARS IN THE INSURANCE INDUSTRY. SHE IS AN ACTIVE COMMUNITY VOLUNTEER. AND IS PASSIONATE ABOUT PEOPLE. HER HEART LOVES TO HELP IN ANY WAY SHE CAN. SHE BELIEVES THAT THE CONNECTIONS WE HAVE TO ONE ANOTHER ARE NOT COINCIDENCES AND IS SO GRATEFUL FOR PEOPLE THAT HAVE COME INTO HER LIFE. SHE BELIEVES IN A LOVING GOD THAT HELPS US ALL THROUGH OUR JOURNEY OF LOVE, TRIALS, GRIEF AND HOPE.

"LET US REMEMBER THOSE WHO DIED AS WELL AS THEIR FAMILIES. THE COURAGE THEY DISPLAYED IN RESPONDING TO A MONSTROSITY OF A SITUATION AND HOW THEY CARRIED OUT THEIR DUTIES WITHOUT HESITATION THOUGHT FOR THEIR OWN SAFETY. THEIR HEROIC FEATS GAVE HOPE TO THOSE TRAPPED INSIDE. YOU THE FIREFIGHTERS OF TODAY ARE THE TRUE KEEPERS OF THE SACRED MEMORY OF THE DEDICATION AND RAW COURAGE AND SACRIFICE OF THE OUTSTANDING HEROES THE SEPT 11, 2001 CARRIED OUT IN THE LINE OF DUTY.

GOD IS THE MASTER OF OUR FATE. HE PREVAILS ABOVE ALL AND CONTINUES TO SHOW HIS PRESENCE EVERY DAY. FF POSSESS THE IDEALS OF LOYALTY, BRAVERY AND DEDICATION FOR THEIR FELLOWMEN. THE FAMILIES OF EACH FALLEN FIREFIGHTER ALSO POSSESS THE SAME BRAVERY AND COURAGE IN REBUILDING THEIR LIVES. THESE ARE NO ORDINARY IDEALS. THEY ARE THE ORDEALS OF GOD. MAY GOD BLESS ALL THE FIRE FIGHTERS AND THEIR FAMILIES."

RETIRED BATTALION CHIEF JOSEPH NARDONE – SPEECH GIVEN AT THE MEMORIAL SERVICE FOR THE 20TH ANNIVERSARY OF 9/11 – 2021

Made in the USA
Las Vegas, NV
26 December 2021